LOOSESTRIFE

ALSO BY STEPHEN DUNN

poetry:

New & Selected Poems, 1974–1994
Landscape at the End of the Century
Between Angels
Local Time
Not Dancing
Work & Love
A Circus of Needs
Full of Lust and Good Usage
Looking for Holes in the Ceiling

prose:

Walking Light: Essays & Memoirs

Stephen Dunn

LOOSESTRIFE

poems

W. W. NORTON & COMPANY

NEW YORK • LONDON

For information about permission to reproduce selections from
this book, write to Permissions, W. W. Norton & Company, Inc.,
500 Fifth Avenue, New York, NY 10110.

The text of this book is composed in Sabon.
Composition by PennSet, Inc.
Manufacturing by the Courier Companies, Inc.
Book design by Beth Tondreau Design

LIBRARY OF CONGRESS CATALOGING-IN-PUBLICATION DATA
Dunn, Stephen, date.
    Loosestrife / Stephen Dunn.
        p.   cm.
    ISBN 0-393-03982-X
    I. Title.
    PS3554.U49L65   1996
    811'.54—dc20   96-1238
                                                        CIP

W. W. Norton & Company, Inc.
500 Fifth Avenue, New York, N.Y. 10110
http://web.wwnorton.com

W. W. Norton & Company Ltd.
10 Coptic Street, London WC1A 1PU

1 2 3 4 5 6 7 8 9 0

FOR DAVE SMITH

Acknowledgments

The following poems have appeared or will appear in these journals:

Antaeus: "The Living"
American Poetry Review: "Aging," "Autocracy,"
   "Because You Mentioned the Spiritual Life"
Atlanta Review: "The Refuge"
Beloit Poetry Journal: "Solving the Puzzle"
CrazyHorse: "Tucson"
Five Points: "This Far Out in the Country"
The Georgia Review: "Named"
The Gettysburg Review: "Responsibility," "Slant"
The Iowa Review: "Grace," "Power"
The Journal of New Jersey Poets: "Disappointment"
Kansas Quarterly: "Opera and Disturbance"
The Marlboro Review: "Paradise"
Mid-American Review: "Poetry," "Radical"
The Nation: "The Fallen World," "Tiger Face"
New England Review: "Heaven," "The Song"
The New Yorker: "Diminuendo"
The Ohio Review: "Ars Poetica"
The Paris Review: "Missing"
Poetry: "After Making Love," "Homage," "Loosestrife,"
   "Meaninglessness," "Nocturne"
The Southern Review: "Imagining Myself My Father,"
   "Road Stop," "The Voice"
Quarterly West: "Criminal"

"Radical" won the James Wright Prize
   from *Mid-American Review*

My thanks to the MacDowell Colony and Yaddo, where several of
these poems were written, and to Richard Stockton College for a series
of summer grants in support of this book. And to all of my faithful
close readers, in particular Lawrence Raab, Philip Booth, Joe-Anne
McLaughlin-Carruth, and my wife, Lois. A special thanks to Carol
Houck Smith for her continuing affection, judgment, and support.

Contents

Solving the Puzzle   *15*

I

Diminuendo   *19*
After Making Love   *21*
Tucson   *22*
Wild   *23*
Paradise   *25*
Heaven   *26*
This Far Out in the Country   *27*
Road Stop   *29*
Slant   *31*
Ars Poetica   *32*

II

Aging   *37*
Nocturne   *38*
The Voice   *40*
Named   *42*
Fibrillations   *44*
Meaninglessness   *46*
The Song   *48*
Missing   *50*
Imagining Myself My Father   *52*

III

The Fallen World   *57*
Grace   *59*
Power   *61*

Seizures   62
Autocracy   63
Responsibility   65
Homage   67
Criminal   68
Poetry   69
Tiger Face   70

IV

The Living   75
Parameters   77
Radical   79
The Refuge   81
Disappointment   83
Because You Mentioned the Spiritual Life   85
Opera and Disturbance   87
Loosestrife   89

Every philosophical catastrophe is a literary opportunity.
—*William Gass*

There are times when we find no warmth in our culture
and then we become a little mad with the desolation of the heart.
—*Martha Graham*

LOOSESTRIFE

Solving the Puzzle

I couldn't make all the pieces fit,
so I threw one away.

No expectation of success now,
none of that worry.

The remaining pieces seemed
to seek their companions.
A design appeared.

I could see the connection
between the overgrown path
and the dark castle on the hill.

Something in the middle, though,
was missing.

It would have been important once.
I wouldn't have been able to sleep
without it.

I

Diminuendo

Everything was clear, and nothing much
   the better for it.
They agreed it was a matter of caring,

and each felt the dull courage that comes
   from caring less.
They weren't going to bring up Avalon,

that shore town where they first met,
   or doing ninety
in the country with the top down:

These were among the unreachables; emblems
   of how they felt
once, about each other and a few

lambent afternoons. They leaned back
   in their chairs
at the café, neither fully present

nor gone, his mind cut loose
   from his heart
like a dinghy in cold, still water.

And she felt the weight of caring
   had been lifted
from her. She felt she would soon know

a freedom some of her friends knew,
   unmoored,
a hundred options in a bittersweet dark.

It was late August. Neither blamed anything
   on how the soul idles
in that relentless hum of days.

Everything's true, they agreed, smiling;
   if something didn't
happen, it certainly would in time.

A black fly landed in her hair, and he
   swept it away.
A sudden breeze uplifted their napkins,

but that was all there was of action.
   It was time to go;
one of them, soon, would say so.

After Making Love

No one should ask the other
"What were you thinking?"

No one, that is,
who doesn't want to hear about the past

and its inhabitants,
or the strange loneliness of the present

filled, even as it may be, with pleasure,
or those snapshots

of the future, different heads
on different bodies.

Some people actually desire honesty.
They must never have broken

into their own solitary houses
after having misplaced the key,

never seen with an intruder's eyes
what is theirs.

Tucson

A man was dancing with the wrong woman
in the wrong bar, the wrong part of town.
He must have chosen the woman, the place,
as keenly as you choose what to wear
when you dress to kill.
And the woman, who could have said no,
must have made her choice years ago,
to look like the kind of trouble
certain men choose as their own.
I was there for no good reason myself,
with a friend looking for a friend,
but I'm not important.
They were dancing close
when a man from the bar decided
the dancing was wrong. I'd forgotten
how fragile the face is, how fists too
are just so many small bones.
The bouncer waited, then broke in.
Someone wiped up the blood.
The woman began to dance
with another woman, each in tight jeans.
The air pulsed. My hands
were fidgety, damp.
We were Mexicans, Indians, whites.
The woman was part this, part that.
My friend said nothing's wrong, stay put,
it's a good fighting bar, you won't get hurt
unless you need to get hurt.

Wild

The year I owned a motorcycle and split the air
in southern Spain, and could smell the oranges
in the orange groves as I passed them
outside of Seville, I understood
I'd been riding too long in cars,
probably even should get a horse,
become a high-up, flesh-connected thing
among the bulls and cows.
My brand-new wife had a spirit
that worried and excited me, a history
of moving on. Wine from a spigot for pennies,
langostinas and angulas, even the language
felt dangerous in my mouth. Mornings,
our icebox bereft of ice,
I'd speed on my motorcycle to the iceman's house,
strap a big rectangular block
to the extended seat where my wife often sat
hot behind me, arms around my waist.
In the streets the smell of olive oil,
the noise of men torn between church
and sex, their bodies taut, heretical.
And the women, elegant, buttoned-up,
or careless, full of public joy, a Jesus
around their necks.
Our neighbors taught us how to close up
in the afternoon,
the stupidity of not respecting the sun.
They forgave us who we were.
Evenings we'd take turns with the Herald Tribune
killing mosquitoes, our bedroom walls bloody
in this country known for blood;
we couldn't kill enough.

When the Levante, the big wind, came out of Africa
with its sand and heat, disturbing things,
it brought with it a lesson, unlearnable,
of how far a certain wildness can go.
Our money ran out. I sold the motorcycle.
We moved without knowing it
to take our quieter places in the world.

Paradise

How attractive trouble feels
in paradise. The place next door
where pain is an option
begins to whisper.
You want the leopard to replace
the swan, the great horned owl
to nudge a songbird out of a tree.
The case for suffering is always
overrated by those whose health
is good, whose houses are calm.
But today you understand
why some people pierce
more than their ears,
why the leisure class has a history
of eating itself from the inside.
And, now, a wish to stir
the stilled air with a serrated knife,
dip into the blackberry jam,
then lick that knife publicly clean,
hoping someone will notice and care.
From the beginning, hasn't it
been the same: the need to woo
a stranger so you'll not be mutinous
alone, to lie down knowingly
among the nettles and the thorns?

Heaven

After the extravagant letter came
　　I remembered how praise
can keep you from belonging to yourself,

and all that afternoon I belonged
　　to some vagrant, sweet,
floating thing. That old daystar, the sun,

turned elsewhere, and the sky darkened
　　as it must.
I lay awake while a light rain fell—

a drummer brushing his drum and tapping
　　the rim.
A rain like that comes from heaven,

my mother would have said, who didn't
　　believe in heaven.
It always made perfect sense,

feeling things at least two ways.
　　I drifted off
hearing my name sung—just the rain,

really, getting insistent, but by then
　　I was near that place
dreamers lean into, baffled, becalmed.

This Far Out in the Country
New Hampshire

Something's wrong for these deer to trust us.
  It's murderous
almost everywhere, and their herd

is too large and, besides, someone always
  has a reason.
At least the yellow-tinged green snake

I saw near the pond where the bullfrogs
  were croaking
knew enough to slither away.

Even the woodchuck on his hind legs
  was brilliantly nervous,
never more than a wobbly dash from his hole.

I remember when outrage came easily,
  and evil's banality
was an insight, not yet a fact.

I remember when white hats beat the black hats
  and got the girls.
I woke this morning from a dream

in which my grandparents were holding hands
  in uneventful moonlight,
city people in a field so large

they appeared lost, though they didn't
  seem to care.
And now these deer, just standing nearby,

not backing off. Perhaps this far out
   in the country
there's a precinct of the charmed.

Wildflowers, sun-touched,
   sway in the wind.
There's a sweet plenitude of air.

Oh, if we didn't know who we are
   and what we've become
we could believe in a paradise

like this, quiescent, inhabited by us . . .

Road Stop

Not all laundromats are sad.
Back in the Village, the one I frequented
was a place to read and watch what women
turn on the delicate cycle for.
I was younger then and wanted to live
in a city, and count myself among
the fashionably poor. Now these women
at The Wash 'N Dry, fingering their coins
in this terrible brightness, just seemed tired.
Maybe all the women back on Bank Street
were tired; I wouldn't have noticed.
Maybe all women everywhere are tired
and even the loveliest, flimsy things
sometimes feel like burdens to take off—
late at night, say, in the wrong mood,
and someone waiting with a smile.
Today these machines look like
the secured masks of deep-sea divers,
and what swirls in them is controlled
confusion, which each of us understands.
I mix my whites and darks together,
as I always do, and a young woman
with a child and a *Live Free Or Die*
T-shirt says No, that's bad.
I tell her I'm interested in speed.
I don't say I've a house
with a washing and drying room, or
my clothes are old enough not to bleed.
Nor do I say I haven't been
to a laundromat in twenty years.
This could be a bus station

the way the solitary faces stare, but she
has a child to scold, no time to stare.
I'm far from home. There's no telling
how I look to those who look so hard
or what, to them, my laundry reveals.
Here's a clean man, they could be thinking.
He must have done something wrong.

Slant

Yesterday, for a long while,
the early morning sunlight
in the trees was sufficient,
replaced by a hello
from a long-limbed woman
pedaling her bike,
whereupon the wind came up,
dispersing the mosquitoes.
Blessings, all.
I'd come so far, it seemed,
happily looking for so little.

But then I saw a cow in a room
looking at the painting of a cow
in a field—all of which
was a painting itself—
and I felt I'd been invited
into the actual, someplace
between the real and the real.

The trees, now, are trees
I'm seeing myself seeing.
I'll always deny that I kissed her.
I was just whispering into her mouth.

Ars Poetica

I'd come to understand restraint
is worthless unless
something's about to spill or burst,

and that the Commandments
understand us perfectly, a large No
for the desirability of everything

vengeful, delicious, out of reach.
I wanted to write ten things
that contained as much.

Maybe from the beginning
the issue was how to live
in a world so extravagant

it had a sky,
in bodies so breakable
we had to pray.

I welcomed, though,
our celestial freedom, our promiscuous flights
all returning to earth.

Yet what could awe us now?
The feeling dies
and then the word.

Restraint. Extravagance. I liked
how one could unshackle the other,
that they might become indivisible.

Astaire's restraint was a kind of extravagance,
while Ginger Rogers danced backwards
in high heels and continued to smile!

She had such grace it was unfair
we couldn't take our eyes off him,
but the beautiful is always unfair.

I found myself imagining him
gone wild, gyrating, leaping,
his life suddenly uncontainable.

Oh, even as he thrashed,
I could tell he was feeling
for limits, and what he could bear.

II

Aging

I tasted and spat
as the experts did
so I could taste again.
I put my nose in. I cleansed
my palate with bread.
A friend guided me;
he thought because I drank often
I drank well.
He thought I might be looking
for subtleties, as he was.
My vocabulary was "good"
and "not so good."
Usually I was a drinker
looking for a mood.
We moved among the oak barrels
and private reserves,
the fine talk of the serious
performing their delicate
mysterious craft.
Yet about the art of aging
I found myself indifferent,
nothing to say or ask.
We went outside,
walked among the woody vines
and fleshy, often violet,
sometimes green, prodigal,
smooth-skinned grapes.
The day was beautiful.
My friend was happy, sated.
There's never enough, I thought.
There never can be enough.

Nocturne

Listening to the inflected quiet
in the woods after a heavy rain—
the steady, lingering emanations
from those intermediaries, the leaves—
he knows he should feel something.

What is tedium? the walls ask.
He thinks it must be
some dullness in himself.
What is solitude? asks the darkness
as it makes its way toward him
through the trees.
He's not sure, but feels
it's having people nearby,
those he's decided not to see.

And remembers the night
he dressed up in funky clothes,
went to a party.
He liked odd hats, oversized ties,
but had forgotten
he was no longer young.
He saw another man like himself.
It was how the lonely dressed.

Next day he told his analyst
he wanted to get in harmony
with his deepest self-deceptions.
"Harmony?" his analyst said,
who tended by temperament
and profession to want to cure,
and so was not useful.

Now, listening to the inflected quiet,
he's struck by how much nature matters
to others. He prefers fine sentences
about digger wasps and tarantulas.
He likes the way a zoom lens
articulates a flower. What would you give
to be perfectly understood? the ceiling says.
Who would want to know me then,
he thinks, who could forgive me?

He realizes that for days now
he hasn't been lying,
but saying other people's truths,
which is worse.
Suddenly to his right,
on the glass table,
there's a monster with a huge head,
powerful wings, several pairs of legs,
moving as if on a vast desert.
A small thing, born to disturb,
the night reveals it for what it is.

The Voice

Just before he woke a voice said,
"You've been a coward
in matters of the heart."
He knew he'd been speaking
to himself, and all day
he felt indicted, caught.
　　　　He went around the house
gluing, banging, rearranging.
Work and the motion of work—
an old therapy, proven, cheap.
Later a storm approached,
melodramatically, as storms do,
his lamp light flickering,
　　　　　　and far off the groan
of a plane, circling, unable
to land. The wind swooshed
in the tall pines. Then came the rain.
In such a storm he wanted someone
to hold, and if allowed
　　　　a further wish
she'd live in his house illusionless
and without excuses
and always respect a good rain enough
to be silent as it fell.
He'd love her better
than anyone he'd loved.
　　　　　　But he was half aware
what dull genius it takes
to deceive yourself this well.
The plane circled lower
and he could hear its single engine,

just one person perhaps trying
to find an opening in the clouds.
He wanted to wish him safely down,
         a him,
he was certain the pilot was a man
with a daily history of tethered freedom
and half-willed despair,
which is why the man flew every chance
there was, even in bad weather.
He felt on the verge of an unseen law;
                    invent,
and some kingdom would open
and there would be its cold chalice
and some lost fundamental news.
Was he fooling himself again?
The thunder had moved way off,
the temperature cooled;
a ghostly steam rose from the grass.
              The voice was no more
than an echo now, a radio wave,
a sound in his head characterized
by a delay. Even as it diminished
it kept meaning the same thing.

Named

He'd spent his life trying to control the names
    people gave him;
oh the unfair and the accurate equally hurt.

Just recently he'd been son-of-a-bitch
    and sweetheart in the same day,
and once again knew what antonyms

love and control are, and how comforting
    it must be to have a business card—
Manager, Specialist—and believe what it says.

Who, in fact, didn't want his most useful name
    to enter with him
when he entered a room, who didn't want to be

that kind of lie? A man who was a sweetheart
    and a son-of-a-bitch
was also more or less every name

he'd ever been called, and when you die, he thought,
    that's when it happens,
you're collected forever into a few small words.

But never to have been outrageous or exquisite,
    no grand mistake
so utterly yours it causes whispers

in the peripheries of your presence—that was
    his fear.
"Reckless"; he wouldn't object to such a name

if it came from the right voice with the right
    amount of reverence.
Someone nearby, of course, certain to add "fool."

After the doctor said not to worry,
there should be a long life ahead of him,
the relief he felt had in it
the disappointment of someone
who'd already imagined himself
the man of brilliant farewells.
Now on his porch,
in the seeming permanence
of the late summer air,
it strikes him that the slow descent
of the sun beneath the trees
has a certain speed.
While there's light
he'd like to see the fox again,
the silver one that appeared
a few dusks ago. He'd like his wife
to see it this time, who thinks—
because of the liar's care he took
describing its tail, its eyes—
that he must have made it up.
But just today coming back
from the doctor's, a turkey vulture,
red-headed and proud, was standing
on a dead cat, roadside,
unmoved by the threat of passing cars.
He told her first about his heart,
then what he'd seen,
which she did not question.
He thinks he must learn to speak
of wild things as if they're secondary;
that must be the key.

Between clouds now, the moon,
and further off a constant flickering.
It's been years
since he's taken the sky personally.
Mosquitoes have begun to insist
the night is theirs. He'll yield to them,
to the unmistakable power of those
aswarm in their numbered hours.
The problem is, no matter what,
always a few follow him inside.
They think he's significant,
a source, perhaps, of small ecstasies.
His wife is reading by lamplight.
They've been married so long
he knows he can tell her the smallest,
stupidest thing, and he does.

Meaninglessness

He was staring at one of its faces,
fine-boned, with one of those faint,
appealing scars, a face he might
seek out at a party on a night
he couldn't help himself again.

He'd learned, but forgotten,
the pointlessness of seeking;
he was, after all, alive,
and desire often sent him aching
toward some same mistake.

The museum was spacious, the walls full
of those gestures toward permanence
he wanted to believe mattered.
No longer was he sure they did.
But he was there, had paid his money.

The definition of beauty, Valéry said, is easy;
it's what leads you to desperation.
He moved from room to room
and the face moved with him.
Renoir's women looked merely healthy.

A museum guard trailed, careful
not to hover. Meaninglessness,
he remembered (but not in time),
is what always makes a promise.
Otherwise we'd expect little

from it, no bloodrush, or grand
holiday of the mind, no sweet
prolonged forgetfulness
about what the future holds, no cheers
from the suddenly awakened soul.

The Song

Late at night a song
breaks off, unfinished,
that rose from the street
outside your apartment,
not a cry but a song,
and something you recognize
as sadness
comes over you.
The street is empty
when you look.
The sadness, too,
is not locatable,
a referent lost somewhere
like an address book
from one of your other lives
with a page missing,
names that must
have mattered once.
A woman was singing
or perhaps a man
with the kind of voice
that has so much woman in it
you should fear for his safety.
The song was familiar,
and it strikes you now
that maybe you were dreaming
or even, yes, it was you
yourself singing.
All night long you wait
for it to start again.
There's only the sound

of cars, and, nearer,
though you can't get that near,
your heart.
You've faked so many feelings
in your time you wonder
if it could have been
the ghost of faked feelings
offering you an authentic sadness,
a gift. But you're so tired,
so on that edge
between clarity and silliness,
you might think anything.
Dawn comes with its intermittency,
its tempo that hasn't
yet lengthened into traffic.
You haven't slept, you swear it,
though you know
when it comes to that
most people are mistaken.

Missing

Frank was missing something,
and women would do anything
to find out what it was.
                    —*James Salter*

He disappeared, often, even as he was speaking,
though he could finish those sentences
from which he had disengaged himself,
finish them well. And when I spoke
he was interested just enough to make me
want to continue speaking. Strange,
that I was flattered by this; it seemed
he was giving me all of half of himself,
the best he could do.
                    In bed, after lovemaking,
which was always good, I knew he'd learned
his post-coital manners—caring, tender—
and was performing them. I was sure
he was planning his next day, his secret
heart checking its secret watch.
I'd known other men like this, of course,
but he was so poor at concealing these faults,
and would admit to them if asked,
they seemed part of his presence, part of
the way he was always *there* for me,
if you know what I mean.
                    I felt, in time,
I could locate, perhaps give life to
his missing half. I felt love could do this.
And I felt even an odd love for his vacancies,
the way, I suppose, most of us will kiss

a terrible scar to prove we can live with it.
He had a good job. Men admired him
because he brought the entire half of himself
to work every day, brought it with intelligence
and charm. It was enough for them.
And all my women friends adored him,
said how lucky I was.
                     But I must admit
it isn't easy to love a man like him.
There's so little asked of you; after a while
you forget you're using half of yourself,
and then something reminds you
and an enormous sense of deprivation follows,
then anger—a quiet fury, I'd call it.
Which is why, finally, I left.
But I've never stopped wondering about him.
And I'm past my anger. If he walked in
right now, I think I'd put my arms around him
and breathe him in, ask him how he was.

Imagining Myself My Father

I drove slowly, the windows open,
letting the emptiness within meet
the brotherly emptiness without.
Deer grazed by the Parkway's edge,
solemnly enjoying their ridiculous,
gentle lives. There were early signs
of serious fog.

Salesman with a product
I had to pump myself up to sell,
merchant of my own hope,
friend to every tollbooth man,
I named the trees I passed.
I knew the dwarf pines,
and why in such soil
they could grow only so tall.

A groundhog wobbled from the woods.
It, too, seemed ridiculous,
and I conjured for it a wild heart,
at least a wild heart.
My dashboard was agleam with numbers
and time.

It was the kind of morning
the dark never left.
The truly wild were curled up, asleep,
or in some high nest looking down.
There was no way they'd let us love them
just right.

I said "fine" to those who asked.
I told them about my sons, athletes both.
All day I moved among men
who claimed they needed nothing,
nothing, at least, that I had.
Maybe another time, they said,
or, Sorry, things are slow.

On the drive back
I drove fast, and met the regulars
at the Inn for a drink.
It seemed to me a man needed a heart
for the road, and a heart for home,
and one more for his friends.

And so many different, agile tongues.

III

The Fallen World

There'd been so much to worry about;
the people couldn't easily forget
the long winters, their violent neighbors
on either side. And the age
of enchantment had passed.
Few sought out the fabulous trials
of slow animals outwitting the swift.
There seemed little need for the sky
to be explained.

Surely this was the fallen world.
And when the blizzard finally subsided,
the soldiers, untamed by story,
decamped and crossed the border.
The soldiers were commited
to only one story, simple and national,
and so took their places in history
among those to whom there's no appeal.

They raped the women
because no story with their shamed faces in it
stood in the way.
They killed some babies
because babies could grow up
and hurt them, their one story said.

The winter ended. Spring came with its sudden
beauty, its warmer weather to kill in,
and the people huddled in their rooms,
furious and afraid.
The children hadn't heard about a princess

or a dragon for months.
They hadn't been delighted into sleep.

They were told one story now, spat out,
whispered, when the soldiers weren't nearby.
It, too, would become their lives.

Grace

After the 1993 World Series

Mulholland extended his hand to Williams,
eased him away from the polite avidity
of reporters—good men mostly,
just doing their jackal job for us.

Didn't we want to know exactly
what public failure felt like?
Mulholland extended his hand
because he couldn't bear what had gone

several questions too long, and Williams,
the wild thing, answering them all straight
down the middle. Mulholland must have known
but for some grace . . . some luck . . .

and how a public man is always a mistake
or two from ruin.
He extended his hand to Williams
while the rest of us watched from our safe

carpeted dens, and the Toronto players
celebrated properly in their locker room.
Back in Jersey, vandals had already thrown eggs
at Williams' house, young men no doubt

without doubt who felt others should die
for them and succeed for them and make them
happy. Oh the luxury of failing in private!
Mulholland extended his hand to Williams

who took it and walked out
of the camera's exacting eye, and into history.
Other teammates, sad themselves,
tried to console him, unsure just then—

as we were—if sympathy could reach
all the hard way to forgiveness.

Power

It comes to this: dwarf-throwing contests,
dwarfs for centuries given away
as gifts, and the dwarf-jokes

at which we laugh in our big, proper bodies.
And people so fat they can't
scratch their toes, so fat

you have to cut away whole sides of their homes
to get them to the morgue.
Don't we snicker, even as the paramedics work?

And imagine the small political base
of a fat dwarf. Nothing to stop us
from slapping our knees, rolling on the floor.

Let's apologize to all of them, Roberta said
at the spirited dinner table. But by then
we could hardly contain ourselves.

Seizures

Some dogs dive under their masters
before they fall, some don't.
One epileptic has his good story
on videotape, his shepherd
suddenly alert as if
waiting for a ball to be thrown,
the timing perfect.
A cruel master, we might suppose,
just hits the floor, recovers to see
his dog curled on the couch.
But my bet is the cruel master
gets saved too.
And the sweetest man on earth
cracks his skull
because his schnauzer hesitates,
though there *are* happy moments
in history, a few.
If I were an epileptic,
or one of us predisposed to fall,
I'd take no chances.
I'd buy a dog of some size
and feed it more than it needs.

Autocracy

After the Chinese movie Raise the Red Lantern

On his property four houses,
one for each mistress.
Red lanterns at dusk
signify which one he'll visit.

No deception needed,
it's his world and this is a tradition.
Among the ruled, though,
the heart's ancient unruliness

as the most intelligent goes mad,
the prettiest takes a lover.
She's hanged in the tower
after the manipulative, jealous one

spreads the secret.
There's an empty house now;
a new girl, serenely attractive,
arrives from the provinces.

The master chooses and presides.
History is his story.
Maybe the sex-starved among us
envy him. Maybe the powerless,

beaten down in third-rate jobs,
dream of such dominion.
But who isn't troubled
by even the simplest union?

Four women in four houses
is a nation.
How quickly it all becomes work,
government.

We should know what he doesn't:
a mistress too long kept waiting
is electricity
before it's been discovered.

In the lanterned courtyard at dusk,
years before Mao and his march
and the terrible remedies,
the unchosen return to their houses.

Responsibility

Last night on Chestnut Neck Road, vandals
used baseball bats on the mailboxes,
selectively it seemed, and our house
was broken into while our old, deaf dog
guarded his sleepfulness.
                        Not much was taken—
it appears they were looking for cash
and settled for a camera, two radios.
But the house was messed up, all except
our daughter's room, which could not be worsened.
    And now all morning
I've been thinking about excuses, the ones
our minds invent to explain
what our bodies have found themselves doing,
and those that arise out of desperation,
fueled by need, legitimate only if we weren't
scoundrels to begin with.

What if they'd spent all week—little
Raskolnikovs—planning something anarchic,
had come armed with a philosophy?
Or what if their motive was a kind of dark joy,
the sheer pleasure of recklessness?
                        Oh vandals,
I can understand, but will not forgive you.
I wish, since they'll let you go if you're caught,
that you would, perhaps, just for me, hurt yourselves,
or, if not for me, out of some ancestral decency
you're suddenly overwhelmed by.
                        I wish
you'd do this in reparation, as a Japanese,

ashamed, might respond to his public failure.
I don't want you to die, just hurt yourselves
in some exactly fair manner. I've nothing
specific in mind, no severing of a finger
or gouging of an eye. You decide.

Homage

Nights when silence gathers
and my old conversation with it
stutters toward a beginning,
usually people are talking
who have no silence in them
and so can leave no mark.
I let it wash over me then.
I say the nothing it hears.

To make the place you live
a vacant place, where nothing happens—
this is how things come to you.
But I do not trust silence
as the saintly do. Sometimes
it smells of its own power
and the dead and the unborn.

I'm turning up the stereo now.
I'm banging a fork against a glass.
Silence loves the moments just after;
its favorite part of a story is the end.
And I, who've so often betrayed it,
wish to please it as much as I can.

Criminal

After Tonya & Nancy

One woman has nothing out of place
as she slides into our living rooms.
The other can't control her face,

the past is in it, and something cheap insists
on the wrong, expensive gowns.
Unnerving, though: nothing out of place.

We know no one is quite that chaste;
always near the palace are the ruins.
The other can't control her face,

yet it's so hard for us to embrace
her, even broken-laced and fallen.
One woman has nothing out of place

and, more unfair, she's all art and excellence.
Turn away, egalitarians.
The other who never learned to control her face

applauds politely, smiles; what grace
she's willed only lasts seconds.
One is beautiful, has nothing out of place.
The other can't control her face.

It makes no difference where one starts,
doesn't every beginning subvert
the tyrannies of time and place?
New Jersey or Vermont, it's the gray zone
where I mostly find myself
with little purpose or design.
An apple orchard, an old hotel—
when I introduce them
I feel I've been taken somewhere
I've been before; such comfort,
like the sound of consecutive iambs
to the nostalgic ear.
Yet it helps as well
here in the middle, somewhat amused,
to have a fast red car
and a winding, country road.
To forget oneself can be an art.
"Frost was wrong about free verse,"
she said to me. "Tear the net down,
turn the court into a dance floor."
She happened to be good looking, too,
which seemed to further enliven her remark.
It always makes a difference
how one ends, aren't endings where you
shut but don't lock the door?
Strange music beginning,
the dance floor getting crowded now.

Tiger Face

Because you can be what you're not
   for only so long,
one day the tiger cub raised by goats

wandered to the lake and saw himself.
   It was astounding
to have a face like that, cat-handsome,

hornless, and we can imagine he stared
   a long time, then sipped
and pivoted, bemused yet burdened now

with choice. The mother goat had nursed him.
   The others had tolerated
his silly quickness and claws.

And because once you know who you are
   you need not rush,
and good parents are a blessing

whoever they are, he went back to them,
   rubbing up against
their bony shins, keeping his secret to himself.

But after a while the tiger who'd found
   his true face
felt the disturbing hungers, those desires

to get low in the reeds, swish his tail,
   charge.
Because he was a cat he disappeared

without goodbyes, his goat-parents relieved
   such a thing was gone.
And we can imagine how, alone and beyond

choice, he wholly became who he was—
   that zebra or gazelle
stirring the great blood rush and odd calm

as he discovered, while moving, what needed
   to be done.

IV

The Living

Our trees limb-heavy and silver—
the beautiful never more on the edge
of breaking—and the indiscriminate
freezing rain slicking
the side streets and back alleys,
the long driveways of the rich.

Nothing moving except kids, the stopped world
just slippery to them, permissive, good.

Our cupboards are near empty.
The liquor cabinet, too.
Under the eaves unfrozen logs
in case the electricity goes.
Bosnians, Sudanese, flicker into our lives,
flicker out. To think of them is to lose
any right to complain.

Will the mail get through? What is uppermost
and most deep down?
I'd like to feel, once again, what I know.

Now a lone car, braving it, going slow,
kids on its fender.
Icicles exclamatory from the shed's roof.
What's underneath is sure
to have something underneath it.
All the way in: that's where crazy is.
The cable's out, or down.
The t.v. screen is snow.

A branch snaps,
and the comparisons that come
are whipcrack, gunshot—the almost dead.
What to do with the barely living
before they die? Exhaust them, I say,
shellac them with our tongues.
Isn't overuse a form of love?
Like a gunshot; like a whipcrack; both,
one last time.

The forecast is more of the same.
And then a few things worse.

I feel like making a little path
from house to car,
then I'm going to scrape.
Wait until it all stops, my wife says.
Is she a realist or an optimist?
I've got my coat on.
I've got the hard-edged shovel in my hand.

North of us, a forest of dwarf pines
visitors always want to see,
miles of coniferous stunted things
and the purest water in the East.

Here, the common gray squirrel,
the banjo-back wood tick.
All of us separating our trash—
no easier way to feel virtuous.

Sunday picnics at the firehouse.
The anydays at the mall.
Half the joggers on Chestnut Neck
have begun to walk

with hand-weights, slowly, their knees gone;
they'll be all forearms soon.
Which one of us isn't trying
to fill up, somehow, our distended days,

our torpid, prime-time nights?
Soon it'll be winter. The underbrush
won't conceal its beer cans,
the collected debris

people have thrown from cars.
We'll feel once again like turning
to our cats, their holy balance
of dignity, wildness.

So much here is unaddressed.
The Gun Club displays its kill.

Racists graffiti the Stop signs.
Curl up with yourselves, we hear

our cats say. Go hesitantly, but go
to others already warm.
Our cats like God have never spoken
a word that wasn't ours.

The marvelous impediment of the ocean
to the east. West: once an entire country
beckoned and promised and stretched.
West: the Port Store, the cranberry bogs.

A few miles south—the White Horse Pike,
casino-marked, parallel to Delilah Road.
Before the dice turned against him,
Rick our good mechanic had his shop there.

Radical

So what if the world's indifferent
spin and tick was a given?
I thought I'd watch the sun climb
the far edge of the ocean,
see if I could break the mindless day
cleanly, my terms, what the hell.

I arrived in the star-filled dark,
found myself remembering
the first time I woke,
astonished,
next to someone beautiful.

Always I wanted to save
the word *magnificent*
for something like that,
for what truly lifts the ceiling.

I sat crosslegged on the sand
in the changing dark.
It announced itself in pink
long before its coming.
Such impertinence, I thought,
like a kid who's just set fire
to his report card, his shame,
outside his teacher's window.

Such brilliance.

Then the gulls began quarreling
as if what was happening

could be a matter of opinion,
but they were mercly experts,
there every morning, not to be trusted.

The Refuge

The snow geese took off in fours,
sometimes in fives, while the great blue heron,
singular and majestically weird,
complicated a rivulet. An egret,
fishing, did its lascivious Groucho Marx
walk, only slowly, neck and head
in odd accord, and hundreds of black ducks,
driven by memory, readied themselves
in the curious calm of New Jersey
for that long flight beyond winter.
                    This was the safe place,
famous for these birds and meetings
of adulterous lovers, everything endangered
protected. Turtle Cove was closed
to humans; the dunlin and the swan
acted as if the world weren't harsh, maniacal.
Absecon Bay stretched out toward the Atlantic,
the very ocean Burt Lancaster said—
with the wild accuracy of a saddened heart—
wasn't the same anymore. The horizon graphed
the ziggy, unequal stretch of casino hotels,
and in front of us on the hard, dirt road
gulls dropped clam shells from a height
so perfect they opened.
                    I had come with my sister-in-law,
nephew and niece, a familial gesture, not exactly
my style. My brother was back on the couch
watching football, my wife cooking
the Thanksgiving dinner that soon would bring us
together. Which one of us didn't need
to be thanked, and eventually forgiven?

A herring gull swallowed an eel.
Walking, the great blue heron
lost all of its grandeur. In a few hours
my brother would say grace at the table,
and we'd bow our heads, almost seriously,
but for now it was red-wing blackbird
and Canada goose, it was marshland and sky,
all the easily praised, the nothing like us.

Disappointment

In this sunlit room with clean sheets,
    a perfect view,
it has a fine place to make its home.

It came with you through the row
    of tollbooths
and over the liberating bridge

with the strange comfort of its
    turned-down smile.
It inhabited the mirror as you drove.

Already the gaiety of the wallpaper
    has begun to disturb.
You open the window to the sea breeze.

You put the black flower in the vase,
    the flower you've imagined.
South Jersey is a place where beauty

is a silent marsh, a blueberry field,
    between the billboards
and the poverty. Beauteous is where you are

if only you hadn't come here.
    There's a mint
on your pillow, a note

from management that insists there's nothing
    that can't be done for you.
Oh, it's so hard to fool disappointment.

It trusts the history of weather
  is on its side.
It wants to give everything its name.

Because You Mentioned
the Spiritual Life

A lone tern turns in the blowsy wind,
and there's the ocean and its timbrous repetitions,
and what a small pleasure it is
that the shade, halfway down,
poorly conceals the lovers next door.
    Fishing boats and sea air,
the moon now on the other side of our world
influencing happiness and crime.
The spiritual life, I'm thinking, is worthless
unless it's another way of having a good time.
        To you I'll say it's some quiet gaiety
after a passage through what's difficult,
perhaps dangerous. I'd like to please you.
So many travelers going to such a small state—
I can see the ferry, triple-tiered and white,
on its way to Delaware.
            I'm peeling and sectioning
an orange. I'm slipping a section into my mouth.
What a perfect thing an orange is
to think about.
                I should say to you
the spiritual life is what cannot be had
through obeisance, but we'll get nowhere
with talk like this.
A darning needle just zoomed by.
The dune grass is leaning west.
                Come join me on the deck,
the gulls are squawking, and an airplane
pulling a banner telling us where to eat

is flying low over the sand castles
and body sculptures the children have built.
The tide will have them soon. Moments
are what we have.

Scrub oaks and black pines,
the Mullica nearby and even nearer
the brackish Nacote Creek,
          in our crawl space
a sump pump and rats' nests,
and up above the tree line
a hawk, common as loneliness
at a party, then a gull riding
downdrafts in the amusement park
of the air,
          every day something
like that above us,
and chiggers, invisible,
in among the ferns, wood ticks
and deer ticks, a paradise
for the insidious,
          after an afternoon
in the garden what lovely monkeys
we become, naked, examining each other
for intruders, what connoisseurs
of the ugly,
          soon tree frogs trilling
in the dark, the bionic raccoon
pushing the cinder block
off the garbage can, and not far off
an expectation of gunshots, screams
from an apartment, our familiar mix
of opera and disturbance,
          titmouse and finch
at the feeder when the sun comes up,
worms comfortable in their slime,

and our regular wakings, sleep-dull faces
in the mirror, the comedy of hours
ahead of us unlived.

Loosestrife

I

Storms moved across the Rockies
and through the plains, rode the jet stream
east. By the time they reached us: rain.
And there were other things that looked—
to other eyes—like welcome news.
The country tilting right.
A few more punishments for the poor.
It was the winter winter never came
to South Jersey; no natural equivalent,
once again, to our lives. All around us
a harshness, a severity, not destined soon
to stop. Oh we were part of it,
reserved ourselves for just a few,
held back instead of gave. Our hearts:
caged things, no longer beating
for the many, who were too many now.
Meanwhile, the Dakotas were snowed in.
A bad wind came off the lakes,
and Chicago and Buffalo braced
for a familiar misery, predictable,
the satisfaction, at least, of what was due.
Here the sun came out and stayed for days.
It wasn't cold enough to think of warmth.
For months, it seemed, we lived lower
in the nation, seasonless, the answers
mostly Christian, though far from Christlike,
to every hard and bitter question.

2

The impatient, upstart crocuses
and daffodils fell once again
for the lies of March.
They simply wanted to exist.
The warm sun must have said Now,
and they gave themselves
to that first, hardly refusable touch.
History was whispering
at least another frost,
but who listens to the hushed sobrieties
of the old? The daffodils died
the advantaged death
of those with other deaths to live.
We stripped down, got colds.
Heraclitus, I want to say I've stepped
into the same stream twice,
and everything felt the same.
It wasn't, I know that now,
but what it felt like
had a truth of its own.
The daffodils and crocuses
traveled through the solitude
of what they felt
toward what they might become.
Choiceless, reactive, inhuman—
nothing to admire in what they did.

3

A superior sky mottled in the west,
the water beneath it glassy, still.
As I crossed the bridge, there it was:

the landscape's invitation to forget.
An osprey swooped low, disreputable
as birds go, but precise, efficient,
a banker in wing-tips, office-bound,
ready to foreclose.
We live in a postcard, I thought,
cropped, agreeably, to deceive;
beyond its edges
broken glass at the schoolyard,
routine boredom, decency, spite.
And then the white, wood-framed
colonials on either side of 575,
Sinton's apple orchard, the shack
with three old cars in front of it,
its porch slanted, no one ever home.
The mowed field and the field wild
with rockrose and goat's rue
declared themselves as property, ours,
no one else's, and I acknowledged
how good the differentiating spaces were
between people and people,
I, who, years ago—
acolyte to an era's pious clarities—
went home to accuse
my dear parents of being capitalists.

4

Clear nights I looked upward and said,
"My God," a figure of speech,
another exhalation of surprise.
The sky was enormous, a planetarium

without walls, the stars free of charge.
Its mythy inhabitants were loose in us,
free-floating energies, nameless now.
It was April, unusually dry.
Forest fires moved through the Barrens.
We needed rain and got wind.
Once we'd have prayed, and gotten wind.
The fires reached Batsto, were stopped
in time, though our time would come.
How to live as if it would? Deeper? Wilder?
Yard sale on Clarks Landing Road.
Raffle at the church. My own yard needing
the care a good citizen would give it.
Thousands of quiet ways gradually to die.
I drove eight miles to the fire's edge.
Planes dropping water had stopped it
and a turn in the wind
and men with shovels and courage.
They didn't need to dig deep, but wide.
It was beyond them, what they had done.

                5

Pascal, even your century compelled you
to feel, "We wander in times not ours."
There were authorities in those days,
there were soul-maps; it's heartening
you knew they couldn't be yours.
Here a four-wheel drive can make it through
our wilderness. The hunter-worn paths
instruct us where to turn. It seems
that much harder to get good and lost.

I dream of the rumored secret road
in Warren Grove, at the end of which
a canoe waits, and miles of winding river.
Dream, too, of the rumored Satanists there
and cats and dogs disemboweled.
I think, Pascal, you would feel
little has changed.
Cherry and apple blossoms can't distract us
long enough, or streets charged
with beautiful body, beautiful face.
Still, I can't be sure, as you were,
that what's hidden is any more mysterious
than the palpable immensity that isn't.

                6

The winter winter never came—like memory
itself—moved from fact to language,
a coloration of what was seen and felt.
My ear still liked winter's doubling.
My eye was fond of its nearness to mistake.
Yet the made world had turned
to the stirrings of grass and insect,
to Oklahoma City bereft.
How little moral effort it takes to open,
then close our hearts! I found myself inclined
now to incident, now to words, conflicted,
like someone besot with spices and sauce,
wishing to stay thin.
The weather urged us out, away from worry,
that indoor work. Cut-offs and rollerblades
met us daringly at the curb, American

as pick-up trucks with rifle racks.
If we walked far enough and looked:
loosestrife, goldenrod, pixie-moss.
I knew loosestrife, I knew so many such things
before I knew their names.

7

Mornings I used to walk the dogs
by Nacote Creek, months before their deaths,
I'd see the night's debris, the tide's vagaries,
the furtive markings of creatures desperate
to eradicate every smell not theirs.
I understood those dogs, who had so little
of their own. Why not perfume
a rock, make a bush a thing redolent
of their best selves? The boat-launch
slanted waterward. The dogs avoided it,
bred for land, doomed to sniff
and cover-up and die—brothers, mine.
This was the town beach, where soon
children would vie with sandpiper and gull.
Every month, like every mind,
changed the way things looked.
I miss those mornings of the dogs.
Winter will be less wind-swept and personal
from now on, spring less observed.

8

Owned by the mayor's brother,
out of earshot of the Zoning Board's

center-of-town houses: The Shooting Place.
Farm-raised quail let loose like mice
for lazy cats, then the shotguns' heavy-metal.
Elsewhere, of course, the quail were kids
who'd gotten in the way of gangs
or their parents' close-quartered rage.
We protested anyway.
In Atlantic City, ten miles southeast,
the marshland gave way to slums
and bright lights. All nature there was human.
The six o'clock news showed the results.
Back here: pitchpine, crowberry, black oak.
Even the directions to The Shooting Place
made us want to say them. Down Chestnut Neck
to Red Wing Lake. Right at the campground.
Gone too far if you reach Beaver Run.

                9

A philosopher, musing cosmically, might think
we were people who needed to be disturbed,
would say no truth ever reveals itself
to those sipping something on their porch.
I hated the cosmic as I hated a big sound
on a quiet afternoon. And I was disturbed enough,
or thought I was, for a hundred truths
to come show their wounded, open hearts.
Where were they then?
Our margaritas were rimmed with salt.
It was 5 p.m. Time even for philosophers—
sure of shelter and sufficient bread—

to take off their shoes, settle in.
Far away, men were pulling bodies from debris,
a moan the sweetest, most hopeful thing.

10

It's been their time—this winter's spring—
the shooters and the complainers
on a side not mine. They wanted America
theirs again, they said, and shouted their votes.
Mice abandoned their ingenious, fluffy homes
in attics and storage rooms, returned
to the fields. Every owl in the county knew.
Everything that couldn't think and everything
that could had made sensible plans.
At school, because it was his bold time,
a home-grown senior hot for elsewhere
asked why I stayed in South Jersey.
"Because it hasn't been imagined yet," I said.
Where he saw nothing, I saw chance.
But I should have said in flat country
friends are mountains, that a place sometimes
is beautiful because of who was good to you
in the acrimonious air. So hard not to lie.
I should have said this landscape,
lush and empty and so undreamed,
is the party to which we bring our own.
I should have kept talking until I'd gotten it true.
Something about what the mouse doesn't know
and the owl does. Something intolerable
like that, with which we live.